# THE ETERNAL EMBER

## A POETRY ON INTERMINABLE HOPE

## SOWPARNIKA NAIR

I dedicate this book to my parents Shynu and Suni, my grandparents Vidyadharan Nair, Ragini, Vasudevan Nair and Kanakavally and to the many mentors that I have had the good fortune of being associated with.

Sowparnika Nair

# Contents

# Contents

# Foreword

In the quiet rhythm of the written word, we often discover the loudest echoes of the human soul. The Eternal Ember is one such exploration, a collection of poems that moves with both grace and gravity across time, place, and emotion. As a reader, you are about to embark on a journey—a journey through lands rich with history, through hearts longing for connection, and through the labyrinth of self-discovery that defines all human experience.

What sets this collection apart is its ability to blend the weight of the past with the lightness of the present, to explore universal truths with intimate language. The poems within these pages do not merely recount moments, they breathe life into them, revealing the layers of feeling that underpin both history and our personal stories. Whether it's the melancholic beauty of Dublin's streets, the haunting pursuit of unachievable love aboard a ship on land, or the ancient wisdom that whispers through the ruins of Taxila, the poems invite us to pause, reflect, and listen to the echoes of the world.

At the heart of these poems lies a deep understanding of the human condition—of love's fleeting nature, of sorrow's enduring shadow, and of the restless search for meaning in the spaces between. The author's words possess a rare quality—simultaneously soft and fierce, tender and relentless. They carry us through vast oceans of thought, offering us fleeting glimpses of the truths that elude us in our waking lives.

It is rare to come across a collection that is as much about the journey as it is about the destination, a journey that traverses both the vastness of the world and the inner landscapes of the heart. The poems in The Eternal Ember are both travelogues and meditations—travelogues that chart journeys to distant lands and meditation on the deep, often unspoken, places within. They speak of our shared history, our endless desires, and the ways in which we, as humans, attempt to make sense of the infinite.

As you turn the pages, let each poem serve as a map, guiding you toward new realms of thought and feeling. Allow the words to bring you closer to understanding not just the world around you, but the world within you. This is not merely a book of poetry, but a quiet companion for those who seek the unspoken truths and untold stories that lie in the heart of every journey.

In these poems, the author offers us more than just their words—they offer us a space to dream, to mourn, to reflect, and to grow. The Eternal Ember is a testament to the power of poetry to transcend time and place, to unite us through our shared human experience, and to leave us, inevitably, changed by the journey. I believe that " The Eternal Ember " resonates with our times and may strike a chord with those who have experienced the challenges of navigating a world where true worth often hides in the shadows.

May you find yourself not just reading these poems, but living within them.

S. Virag

# Preface

Poetry, at its heart, is a map of the soul's landscape—sometimes jagged, often serene, but always true to the emotions that stir within. In The Eternal Ember, I invite you to travel through realms of mind, reality, history and landscapes both real and imagined, and the quiet corners of the heart that pulse with longing and reflection. This collection is a tapestry of experiences—some inspired by the world we live in, and others by the world we dream of, woven together through verses that stretch from the shores of Dublin to the deserts of Taxila, from the solitude of a ship sailing on land to the eternal struggle between unrequited love and the yearning for understanding.

The poems in this book reflect the complexities of human existence—the highs and lows, the victories and losses, and the endless search for meaning. From the melancholic hum of Dublin's streets to the sorrowful yet resilient journey of a ship seeking love in lands unknown, these poems seek to explore the infinite expanse of the human experience. They celebrate the beauty of the world, even as they grapple with the pain and beauty that comes from loss, longing, and the elusive nature of connection.

Each poem serves as a passage—a step in a deeper exploration of what it means to world, to hope, to dream, and to ultimately understand the truth that lies beyond the tangible. Whether it is the sun-drenched shores of the Galapagos, the echo of ancient wisdom in Taxila, the silent spaces of Jerusalem, or the heartbreak of love that cannot be reached, this collection is a journey through the landscape of our minds, our history, and our desires.

I have always believed that poetry is not just about capturing moments but about transporting us to other worlds, to realms where the impossible becomes possible, and where the heart can speak its truest desires. As you read these poems, I hope you find within them echoes of your own unspoken thoughts, your quiet dreams, your struggles, and your moments of peace.

The Eternal Ember is my attempt to capture fleeting glimpses of beauty, to make sense of the contradictions and complexities of our existence, and to remind you, dear reader, that even in the darkest corners, there is light to be found—whether in the city streets of Dublin, the ruins of Taxila, or in the eternal voyage of a ship sailing in search of something it can never fully attain. May this book serve as both a journey and a reflection.

Sowparnika Nair

# Acknowledgements

This book is the culmination of countless moments of inspiration, reflection, and support from those who have walked alongside me, both near and far. As I put these words into the world, I am deeply grateful to the people and places that have shaped this collection and made it possible. To my family, whose unwavering love and encouragement have been my anchor, I owe everything. Your faith in me, even when I doubted myself, gave me the courage to put my thoughts into words and my words into this book. You are the heart of my inspiration and the quiet strength behind my work.

To the countless poets, writers, and storytellers who have come before me—thank you for showing me the boundless possibilities of language. James Joyce, Oscar Wilde, and the great epic poets of history, your words have been a guiding light, illuminating the path for my own.

A heartfelt thanks to my teachers, friends and mentors, who read early drafts, shared kind words, and provided invaluable feedback. To the readers, who will bring these poems to life with their own interpretations and emotions, thank you.

Sowparnika Nair

# 1. The Eternal Ember

*In a world turned topsy-turvy, strange to see,*
*Where skills esteemed dissolve like morning haze,*
*The wise, puzzled, wear silence irony,*
*While empty rote prevails in learning maze.*
*The diligent, like whispers in the breeze,*
*Find fruits denied, knowledge tossed away,*
*Yet those who echo with practical ease,*
*Reap unearned praise in this odd, skewed display.*
*Despair may visit capable hearts, true,*
*As merit and progress lose their way,*
*Shallow applause claims centre, but we knew,*
*The gifted, adrift, in silent dismay.*
*But still a glimmer shine amid the gloom,*
*Changes' winds may rise, dispelling the fume.*

# 2. Echoes of Doubt

*In shadows deep, where whispers breed,*
*Conspiracy's tangled web takes seed.*
*In hushed tones, tales are spun,*
*Of secrets kept from everyone.*
*A world beneath the world we know,*
*Where truth is veiled, and lies can grow.*
*Mysteries cloaked in cloak and hood,*
*In the dark, they understood.*
*They say the moon is made of cheese,*
*And aliens dance with such ease.*
*They speak of hidden government plots,*
*And clandestine meetings in shadowed spots.*
*From Roswell's crash to the moon's dark side,*
*Conspiracies in the night abide.*
*Theories spun, like a spider's thread,*
*Weaving doubt in each word said.*
*Yet amidst the chaos and the doubt,*
*Some kernels of truth may eke out.*
*For even in the strangest tale,*
*There may be truth that will prevail.*
*So listen close, but with discerning ear,*
*For truth and falsehood often near.*

*Conspiracies may come and go,*
*But truth, in time, will always show.*

# 3. Casting Shadows

*In halls of power, nepotism's reign,*
*Where favour flows through kinship's chain.*
*Connections forged in blood and name,*
*Eclipsing merit, feeding fame.*
*The throne of opportunity, it seems,*
*Reserved for those in privileged dreams.*
*While talent waits in silent plea,*
*Bound by nepotism's decree.*
*Inheritance of privilege, stark and clear,*
*As the chosen rise without a fear.*
*Doors swing wide for the favoured few,*
*Leaving others to the residue.*
*Yet merit, like a seedling small,*
*May struggle, but it stands tall.*
*Against the tide of biased choice,*
*It raises its voice, finds its voice.*
*For nepotism's grip may hold fast,*
*But fairness lingers, built to last.*
*In the end, it's talent's flame,*
*That truly ignites the game.*
*So let us strive for fairness true,*
*Where merit shines, and dreams accrue.*

*And may nepotism's hold relent,*
*In a world where all talents are content.*

# 4. Digital Dance

*In the realm where screens hold sway,*
*The echoes of our words betray.*
*A world of likes and shares, we roam,*
*Yet wisdom oft finds little home.*
*Through filters bright and polished lies,*
*We seek approval 'neath digital skies.*
*In endless scrolls of endless streams,*
*Reality fades, lost in the gleam.*
*The folly of our digital dance,*
*Where shallow words hold shallow stance.*
*In memes and tweets, we find our voice,*
*Yet substance fades, drowned in noise.*
*In the quest for hearts and thumbs,*
*We sacrifice depth for fleeting sums.*
*Connections made in binary code,*
*Yet loneliness lingers, a heavy load.*
*In the mirror of our screens, we see,*
*The folly of our vanity.*
*For in the glow of digital light,*
*We lose ourselves, lose our sight.*
*So let us pause, and take heed,*
*In this digital age of speed.*

*For wisdom's voice, though often quiet,*
*Is drowned by the roar of digital riot.*

# 5. Voyage of Knowledge

*In search of knowledge, far and wide,*
*We journey forth with hearts untied.*
*From distant lands to foreign shores,*
*Seeking wisdom's boundless stores.*
*Across the seas, across the skies,*
*Educational migration flies.*
*In classrooms new, we find our place,*
*Amidst the beauty of diverse grace.*
*Leaving behind the familiar embrace,*
*We embrace the challenge; we embrace the chase.*
*For in the pursuit of learning's flame,*
*We find a world without a name.*
*Cultures clash and merge as one,*
*In the melting pot beneath the sun.*
*Ideas bloom, perspectives grow,*
*As educational currents flow.*
*From east to west, from north to south,*
*We trace the lines of knowledge's mouth.*
*For in the tapestry of human quest,*
*Educational migration finds its rest.*
*So let us celebrate the journey's song,*
*As we travel forth, brave and strong.*

*For in the pursuit of wisdom's glow,*
*Educational migration helps us grow.*

# 6. Democracy

*In today's world, democracy's song,*
*Echoes loud, yet wrought with wrong.*
*A fragile dance of power and voice,*
*Where freedom's flame finds constant choice.*
*In the tumult of divisive cries,*
*Democracy weaves through truth and lies.*
*A battlefield where ideals clash,*
*In the pursuit of a brighter path.*
*From ballot boxes to digital screens,*
*Where voices rise and echo dreams.*
*Yet shadows lurk in corridors deep,*
*Where power's grip may silence sleep.*
*In the streets where protests swell,*
*Democracy's heartbeat loudly tells,*
*Of voices rising, refusing to yield,*
*In the face of injustice's shield.*
*But democracy's promise, though grand,*
*Requires vigilance, a guiding hand.*
*For in the currents of today's strife,*
*It's the people who must shape their life.*
*So let us cherish this fragile flame,*
*And guard against those who seek to maim.*

*For in the heart of democracy's call,*
*Lies the hope for freedom for one and all.*

# 7. Solitude in Albuquerque

*In Albuquerque's quiet streets they tread,*
*Single men with thoughts unsaid.*
*Beneath the glow of neon light,*
*In solitude, they roam the night.*
*Deserted alleys, whispers low,*
*Echoes of a city's ebb and flow.*
*Footsteps soft on pavement bare,*
*In the stillness, they're the only pair.*
*Each shadowed corner holds a tale,*
*Of solitary souls who never fail,*
*To wander through the city's veins,*
*Seeking solace from their pains.*
*In the silence, they find their peace,*
*As the city's pulse begins to cease.*
*Albuquerque's streets, deserted, wide,*
*With single men, they quietly bide.*
*But in their solitude, there lies a grace,*
*A quiet strength, a hidden place.*
*For in the heart of the empty street,*
*Lies the echo of their silent beat.*

# 8. Dublin Lights

*In Dublin's streets, where shadows dance,*
*Echoes of Joyce's Dubliners entrance.*
*A city of tales, both joy and woe,*
*Where characters' lives ebb and flow.*
*Beneath the watchful eye of Molly Malone,*
*The city's heartbeat is felt alone.*
*In cobblestone lanes, history weaves,*
*Through every corner, every eave.*
*From Lenehan's wanderings in the night,*
*To Gabriel's introspective plight,*
*Dublin's stories, rich and vast,*
*In Joyce's words, they forever last.*
*The Liffey flows, a ribbon of time,*
*Reflecting Dublin's prose sublime.*
*Each pub a stage for stories told,*
*In voices young, and voices old.*
*In the laughter of the Hynes family's feast,*
*Or the silent tears of Eveline, released,*
*Dublin's soul is bared and true,*
*In Joyce's Dubliners, through and through.*
*So let us wander Dublin's streets,*
*Where history and fiction meet,*

*And in Joyce's novel, we find a key,*
*To unlock the city's mystery.*

# 9. The Silent Sea

*Alone amidst the vast expanse,*
*A solitary soul, in solitude's trance.*
*In the middle of the sea, where silence reigns,*
*Echoes of loneliness, no comfort gains.*
*The endless horizon, a circle unbroken,*
*A heart adrift, with words unspoken.*
*No land in sight, no friendly face,*
*Just endless waves, in their relentless chase.*
*The sky above, vast and grey,*
*Reflecting the melancholy of the day.*
*A solitary gull, its cry a mournful song,*
*As the lonely hours stretch out long.*
*In the middle of the sea, where time stands still,*
*Solitude wraps around like a chill.*
*No footsteps mark the sands of time,*
*Just the rhythm of waves, a lonely rhyme.*
*But in the solitude, a whisper soft and low,*
*A reminder that even in the depths, we grow.*
*For amidst the loneliness, a strength is found,*
*In the heart of silence, a soul profound.*
*So let the sea embrace, let solitude console,*
*In its quiet depths, find peace in the whole.*

*For in the middle of the sea, beneath the sky so wide,*
*Solitude becomes a friend, a companion by your side.*

# 10. The Trader of Emotions

*In the market's dance of bulls and bears,*

*A trader's heart knows countless cares.*

*Emotions whirl like leaves in the wind,*

*As fortunes rise and others rescind.*

*At dawn's first light, with hope aglow,*

*They watch the ticker's ebb and flow.*

*Anticipation quickens every breath,*

*As they navigate the dance of life and death.*

*With every rise, euphoria's high,*

*Their dreams take flight, they touch the sky.*

*But in the blink of an eye, fortunes turn,*

*And fear's cold grasp begins to churn.*

*Anxiety grips, as losses mount,*

*Their hopes and dreams begin to count.*

*They watch the numbers with bated breath,*

*Wondering what comes after this test of faith.*

*Yet amidst the chaos, a calm may rise,*

*As wisdom dawns in seasoned eyes.*

*For in the market's tumultuous sea,*

*A trader finds resilience, a will to be free.*

*So they weather the storms, they ride the waves,*
*Knowing that in every loss, there's a chance to pave,*
*A path anew, with lessons learned,*
*In the ever-changing tides, their fire still burned.*

# 11. Echoes of Deception

*In the age of information, where truth's thin thread is spun,*
*The rise of fake news casts shadows 'neath the sun.*
*In every corner of the digital domain,*
*Falsehoods spread like wildfire, feeding on the pain.*
*It starts with a click, a headline bold and bright,*
*Drawing eyes like moths to the flame's deceitful light.*
*Sensational tales, with kernels of truth entwined,*
*Captivate the mind, leaving reason far behind.*
*In the echo chambers of the online sphere,*
*False narratives echo loud and clear.*
*Opinions masquerade as facts, unchecked and wild,*
*As misinformation spreads like a virus, defiled.*
*From political agendas to health's sacred ground,*
*Fake news knows no bounds, no virtue found.*
*Conspiracy theories weave their tangled web,*
*Capturing hearts and minds, leading them to ebb.*
*But amidst the chaos, a glimmer of hope may shine,*
*As truth seekers rise, their voices intertwined.*
*Fact-checkers labour, in the trenches deep,*
*To debunk falsehoods and awaken minds from sleep.*
*Yet the battle rages on, a relentless fight,*
*As fake news proliferates, day and night.*

*In the quest for truth, we must remain vigilant and bold,*
*For in the war against falsehoods, truth will always hold.*
*So let us arm ourselves with knowledge and with care,*
*And discern the truth from lies, in the digital glare.*
*For in the age of fake news, truth's light must shine,*
*Guiding us through the darkness, to a future divine.*

# 12. Masked Shadows

*In shadows deep, where masks adorn,*
*Fake souls weave their web of scorn.*
*With honeyed words and smiles feigned,*
*Their deceitful dance, by truth, is stained.*
*Beneath the guise of friendship's art,*
*Lies a hollow core, devoid of heart.*
*Their presence lingers, a toxic stain,*
*Leaving wreckage in their selfish gain.*
*But beware, for truth's light shall reveal,*
*The falsehoods hidden, the wounds they deal.*
*For in the end, their façade will crack,*
*And their deceitful ways shall not lack.*
*So to the fake, with hearts of stone,*
*Know that your charade will soon be known.*
*For authenticity reigns in the end,*
*And in its glow, fake souls descend.*

# 13. The World I Never Travelled

*There lies a world I've never seen,*
*Where oceans whisper, forests gleam.*
*Mountains rise with skies so wide,*
*And mysteries dwell where shadows hide.*
*Its streets are paved with untold tales,*
*Of desert winds and Arctic gales.*
*Its rivers hum a tune unknown,*
*A melody etched in lands I've not flown.*
*A dawn breaks soft on foreign shores,*
*A twilight sings where silence pours.*
*The stars align in patterns rare,*
*Their secrets lost to the paths I don't dare.*
*Fields of flowers with colours untamed,*
*Whisper stories they've never named.*
*And castles crumble in quiet grace,*
*Hiding the echoes of a time and place.*
*I dream of faces I'd never greet,*
*And languages sung in markets and streets.*
*Of hands that build and hearts that bind,*
*In a world I'll never leave behind.*

*But though my feet may not wander far,*
*My heart has travelled where dreams are.*
*And in the mapless, boundless skies,*
*The world I never travelled lies.*

# 14. The Pilgrims of the Sky

*Upon the winds where the salt spray flies,*
*Beneath vast arcs of Atlantic skies,*
*The pilgrims of feathers take their flight,*
*Through endless days and starry night.*
*From northern fjords, where the glaciers gleam,*
*And rivers pour like a silver stream,*
*They lift their wings to the call of the seas,*
*Drawn by whispers of oceanic breeze.*
*The Atlantic spreads, a mighty road,*
*Where no compass or map has ever showed.*
*Yet, they journey across its cobalt span,*
*In rhythms older than time began.*
*Far south they aim, where the warmth does call,*
*To hidden isles where the sunlight falls.*
*And there, like a sentinel, silent and grand,*
*Rests Napoleon Island, carved by hand—*
*Not of men, but time, and wind, and wave,*
*A refuge eternal, a fortress brave.*
*The terns, with cries like a piercing song,*
*Skim the waters, sharp and strong.*

*Their journey spans a hemisphere wide,*
*Chasing the summer, defying the tide.*
*From Arctic ice to Antarctic glow,*
*Through storms where only the fearless go.*
*The shearwaters glide, with wings so thin,*
*Drawn to the ocean's rhythmic hymn.*
*Through endless currents and surging streams,*
*They follow the pull of ancient dreams.*
*And when they rest on Napoleon's shore,*
*Their stories mingle with the island's lore.*
*Napoleon Island, lonely and free,*
*A jewel afloat in the vast blue sea.*
*Its cliffs rise stark, where the albatross weaves,*
*And the winds hum soft through the tufts of leaves.*
*Here, time slows down, and silence sings,*
*A haven of peace for the wanderers' wings.*
*The Atlantic dances with shifting moods,*
*In tempests wild, or gentle interludes.*
*The birds endure its icy breath,*
*Risking the spectre of watery death.*
*Yet onward they press, through spray and foam,*
*For instinct drives them to their home.*
*The gannets plunge like arrows keen,*
*In dazzling dives, their grace is seen.*
*They pierce the waves with deadly art,*
*To reap the gifts the ocean imparts.*
*And by Napoleon's weathered stone,*

*They rest, united, never alone.*
*The Atlantic tells of journeys vast,*
*Of creatures fleeting, shadows cast.*
*A highway eternal, a liquid stage,*
*For migrations timeless, age upon age.*
*Through its heart, the winged ones soar,*
*Bound by the tides to every shore.*
*And as the pilgrims return each year,*
*The world takes note, both far and near.*
*For their flight, so fragile, yet bold and wise,*
*Reminds us all to lift our eyes—*
*To see the ocean not as a divide,*
*But as the thread where worlds collide.*
*Napoleon Island stands as a mark,*
*A beacon of hope in waters dark.*
*And in its shadow, they come to rest,*
*The birds of the Atlantic, nature's best.*
*Their journeys written on winds that wail,*
*A testament to life's enduring trail.*

# 15. The Sea at Kanyakumari

*Where three great waters converge and meet,*
*At India's edge, where the land retreats,*
*The sea at Kanyakumari sings,*
*Of timeless truths and eternal things.*
*The Bay of Bengal, in its restless flow,*
*Meets the Arabian Sea, where warm winds blow,*
*And the Indian Ocean, vast and wide,*
*Mingles their tides on this southern side.*
*The sun rises here in a crimson hue,*
*Painting the waves with a golden view.*
*The dawn is born where the oceans play,*
*And whispers of night dissolve with the day.*
*The fishermen cast their nets with care,*
*As morning breathes its salt-filled air.*
*Their boats, like specks, on the horizon sway,*
*Dancing to tides that never delay.*
*The Vivekananda Rock stands tall,*
*A temple of thought, embracing all.*
*Its stone remembers the sage's quest,*
*The meditations of a soul at rest.*

*The sea around it, fierce yet serene,*
*Guards the wisdom that lies between.*
*The goddess watches, her gaze afar,*
*Kumari Amman, like a guiding star.*
*Her legend weaves with the ocean's lore,*
*A virgin's vow on this sacred shore.*
*The waves that kiss her temple's feet,*
*Carry devotion, vast and deep.*
*By day, the sea shimmers azure bright,*
*Its depths a mirror of the heavens' light.*
*The sunlit waters, playful and free,*
*Hold secrets buried in eternity.*
*And yet, as evening begins its descent,*
*The colors of twilight are silently spent.*
*The sunset at Kanyakumari glows,*
*As the western sky in amber flows.*
*The horizon burns in fiery hues,*
*A fleeting beauty, nature's muse.*
*The waves reflect the fading light,*
*And gently embrace the coming night.*
*When darkness falls, the sea still sings,*
*A lullaby borne on the wind's soft wings.*
*Its rhythm endless, its voice profound,*
*A hymn of life in its ceaseless sound.*
*Stars awaken and glimmer above,*
*Their silver gaze a sign of love.*
*The lighthouse beams its steady light,*

*A guardian piercing the velvety night.*
*It warns the ships of the rocky embrace,*
*Of waters that hide their dangerous face.*
*Yet, even in peril, the sea remains,*
*A teacher of courage, joy, and pain.*
*In monsoons wild, the waves will rise,*
*Thunderous, roaring to stormy skies.*
*Yet, when the tempest fades away,*
*Peace returns like a child at play.*
*The cycle continues, fierce and calm,*
*A symphony sung in the ocean's palm.*
*The sea at Kanyakumari speaks to the soul,*
*Of journeys unfinished, of being whole.*
*It tells of endings that lead to starts,*
*Of the meeting of worlds, of joining hearts.*
*Its vastness whispers, "You are free,*
*To dream as deep as the boundless sea."*
*Here, where waters three unite,*
*Kanyakumari holds its light.*
*A place where earth and sea conspire,*
*To stir the heart and inspire desire.*
*To stand at the edge, where horizons blend,*
*And feel the infinite—without end.*

# 16. Cape of Good Hope: A Sailor's Lament

*Beneath the skies where storms convene,*
*And oceans churn in shades unseen,*
*Lies the Cape of Good Hope, bold and vast,*
*A sentinel shaped by time's rough cast.*
*The edge of Africa, wild and steep,*
*Where dreams have wandered and waters weep.*
*Through tempest winds and surging tides,*
*Sailed men with courage, yet hearts that cried.*
*The ships they steered with timbered grace,*
*Carried the hope of a far-off place—*
*India's riches, her spices and gold,*
*A paradise sought by the brave and bold.*
*From Lisbon's harbours, under starry shrouds,*
*Or Venice, cloaked in evening clouds,*
*They left their homes, their loves, their kin,*
*To face the trials of the seas within.*
*The salty breeze and the ocean spray*
*Pulled them farther from those they'd obeyed.*
*At the helm stood dreams both bright and stark,*
*Guided by stars in the endless dark.*

*But when the nights grew cold and long,*
*Melancholy hummed its sober song.*
*The waves would whisper of lands afar,*
*While hearts would ache for a hearthside star.*
*"Does my child remember my face?" they'd sigh,*
*As the moon hung low in the weeping sky.*
*"Does my wife still pray by the firelight's glow,*
*While I sail through waters I do not know?*
*Will these winds that rage and groan,*
*Lead me back to the life I've known?"*
*They passed the Cape, where the tempests roar,*
*Where legends rise from the ocean's core.*
*Bartholomeu Dias first braved its might,*
*Naming it 'Good Hope' in the pale moonlight.*
*Yet many would fall to its wrathful gales,*
*Their stories swallowed by sorrowed wails.*
*The Cape of Storms, as the sailors declared,*
*Was a place where both courage and fear were barred.*
*Its cliffs stood high, like a judgment throne,*
*Marking the place where the lost are known.*
*The sirens sang with a haunting grace,*
*And pulled the weary to their watery place.*
*For Vasco da Gama, the journey was true,*
*He crossed the Cape and the heavens' blue.*
*To Calicut's shores, where the spices lay,*
*He found the India for which they'd prayed.*
*But what of the men who had paid the cost?*

*Their bones lie deep where the waves are tossed.*
*By firelight in Europe, their loved ones wept,*
*As the years grew long and promises slept.*
*Sailors wrote letters that would never return,*
*Words of longing in pages that burned.*
*"Though India's wealth may line the King's crown,*
*What use is gold when the soul breaks down?"*
*The Cape of Good Hope, both cruel and kind,*
*Was a place of dreams and hearts confined.*
*For every man who saw it through,*
*A hundred fell to the ocean's blue.*
*And those who lived bore the scars of the deep,*
*A haunting grief that would never sleep.*
*The waves at the Cape still crash and moan,*
*Echoing voices of men long gone.*
*The winds still whisper of wives and sons,*
*Of villages quiet when the day is done.*
*And though the world has shifted since then,*
*The Cape remembers the hearts of men.*
*So raise a toast to those who braved,*
*The raging storms, the lives they gave.*
*To the Cape of Good Hope, a threshold vast,*
*A monument to the sailors' past.*
*For in their grief and courage combined,*
*We find the essence of humankind.*

# 17. Calicut: The Sailor's Solace

*I came to Calicut on restless seas,*
*A sailor drawn by the spice-laden breeze.*
*From Europe's shores, cold and grey,*
*To this golden land where the palms sway.*
*The waves that bore me whispered tales,*
*Of fragrant winds and silken sails,*
*Of Calicut's shores, a beacon bright,*
*Where east and west unite in light.*
*The port was alive with a timeless tune,*
*Of bustling trade beneath the monsoon.*
*Merchants shouted, their wares displayed—*
*Pepper, cardamom, silk finely laid.*
*The scent of cloves hung thick in the air,*
*A treasure trove beyond compare.*
*Here, in this city by the Malabar tide,*
*I found a world where dreams reside.*
*Time passed like the ebb of the seas,*
*And Calicut became a home to me.*
*I left behind Europe's distant shore,*
*To walk these streets and seek no more.*

*But in quiet hours, beneath the moon's glow,*
*Memories of the past would softly flow.*
*Of lands I'd known and kin I'd lost,*
*Of dreams fulfilled at a sailor's cost.*
*In the heart of Calicut, there lies a lane,*
*Known as SM Street, a timeless refrain.*
*It buzzes with life, yet whispers the past,*
*Where footsteps linger, memories last.*
*By day it glows in a vibrant stream,*
*Shops and stalls, a merchant's dream.*
*By night, its silence hums with lore,*
*Of the city's glory in days of yore.*
*I wander its path, as shadows grow tall,*
*Hearing the echoes of a distant call.*
*I see the traders from lands far and wide,*
*With ships anchored close to the Malabar tide.*
*The Portuguese, the Arabs, the Chinese too,*
*Their voices mingling as breezes blew.*
*I see myself, a stranger then,*
*Lost in this market, amidst its din.*
*SM Street is more than a bustling lane;*
*It's a keeper of stories, of joy and pain.*
*The cobblestones murmur of lives once known,*
*Of sailors, merchants, a city grown.*
*I hear the laughter of children's play,*
*The cries of hawkers at the break of day.*
*The scent of sweets from halwa stalls,*

*The rhythm of life in its narrow walls.*
*Yet, the people who gather here today,*
*Long for the Calicut of a bygone day.*
*They speak of kings and Zamorin's pride,*
*Of ships that sailed with the rising tide.*
*They mourn the loss of the city's grace,*
*Of simpler times in this bustling space.*
*And I, though now a part of this land,*
*Feel the weight of history's hand.*
*Calicut, oh Calicut, cradle of trade,*
*Your shores are where destinies were made.*
*The spice-scented winds that kissed my face,*
*Still carry the soul of this sacred place.*
*Though the world has changed, your heart remains,*
*In SM Street's laughter, its joys and pains.*
*I, the sailor who found his home,*
*Am no longer lost, no longer alone.*
*Now, as I walk by this vibrant street,*
*I hear the past in every heartbeat.*
*The rhythm of drums, the clang of bells,*
*The salty air with its ancient spells.*
*This city, this lane, they breathe as one,*
*Beneath the gaze of the setting sun.*
*And though the world may forget your lore,*
*Calicut, your spirit will endure evermore.*

# 18. The Immortal Warrior

*Born beneath the stars of Utharashada's light,*
*Where virtues rise like mountains in the night,*
*Ashwatthama came with a cosmic flame,*
*A name of thunder, a soul untamed.*
*The son of Drona, the sage of might,*
*Destined for war, yet bound by the right.*
*Under the heavens where dharma reigns,*
*He was forged in the fire of celestial veins.*
*The Utharashada, bright and high,*
*Marks the warrior who never will die.*
*A star of truth, of courage and zeal,*
*A symbol of strength, of hearts like steel.*
*Those born of its rays are steady and strong,*
*Resolute seekers of right and wrong.*
*And so was Ashwatthama, bold and wise,*
*With a heart that burned like the eternal skies.*
*From the moment his first cry split the air,*
*A cosmic blessing was his to bear.*
*Born with a gem upon his brow,*
*A mark of power, of destiny's vow.*
*The gods themselves blessed this child,*
*A warrior fierce, both calm and wild.*

*The blood of sages, the strength of kings,*
*Flowed through his veins like sacred springs.*
*With Drona's guidance, his skill took flight,*
*An archer supreme, unmatched in fight.*
*He learned to wield the bow with grace,*
*And strike his foes in the fiercest chase.*
*The Brahmastra's wisdom he held in hand,*
*A gift from his father, a force to command.*
*In every battle, his name would roar,*
*The might of Ashwatthama, the eternal lore.*
*When Kurukshetra's fields turned red,*
*With cries of the dying, the blood of the dead,*
*Ashwatthama stood as a blazing flame,*
*Fighting for honour, defending his name.*
*The Pandavas feared his fiery might,*
*For none could match him in the fight.*
*The power of Utharashada burned in his soul,*
*A warrior destined to conquer his goal.*
*His arrows sang with a deadly tune,*
*Piercing shadows beneath the moon.*
*His chariot raced like a tempest's gale,*
*Through storm and fury, he'd never fail.*
*Each strike he made, a hymn to war,*
*A son of the stars, born to soar.*
*Even Arjuna, with his Kshatriya pride,*
*Felt the weight of Ashwatthama's tide.*
*Yet the heart of the warrior bore a scar,*

*For dharma in war is ever bizarre.*
*His loyalty to Duryodhana bound his way,*
*Though his conscience wrestled with him each day.*
*For Ashwatthama, the star-born knight,*
*Knew the path of dharma wasn't always bright.*
*And in his wrath, when his father fell,*
*A rage awakened, as fierce as hell.*
*Beneath the star of Utharashada's lore,*
*Is the truth that burns at the very core:*
*Unyielding resolve, but a heavy price,*
*A warrior's dharma is sacrifice.*
*In the night of vengeance, his hand did stray,*
*When the sons of the Pandavas met his blade's sway.*
*The immortal flame within his heart,*
*Turned to ash, as he tore it apart.*
*The curse of Krishna was a weight to bear,*
*To walk the earth in eternal despair.*
*Yet even in exile, his might remains,*
*A wanderer bound by immortal chains.*
*For Utharashada, steadfast and true,*
*Keeps his spirit burning, ever anew.*
*The warrior's soul, though battered and torn,*
*Carries the fire of the star he was born.*
*Ashwatthama, the gem-crowned flame,*
*Will forever live in the Mahabharata's name.*
*A warrior peerless, a soul profound,*
*In the annals of time, his name resounds.*

*Though dharma's path is jagged and steep,*
*His legend is one the stars will keep.*
*For beneath Utharashada's guiding light,*
*Ashwatthama remains a force of might.*
*A seeker of truth, of victory's glow,*
*A symbol of strength in life's ebb and flow.*
*Immortal in pain, immortal in lore,*
*The greatest warrior, forevermore.*

# 19. The Father of the Free

*In the quiet hills where the Potomac flows,*
*There stands a home where history glows,*
*Mount Vernon, his countryside grace,*
*A reflection of a leader's steadfast embrace.*
*George Washington, the father, the guide,*
*With roots in England and dreams wide,*
*He forged a path in the New World's land,*
*A visionary with a steady hand.*
*But long before the American fields,*
*Before freedom rang with triumphant peals,*
*In Sulgrave Manor, across the sea,*
*Lies the origin of his family tree.*
*In the English shire of Northampton's fold,*
*A modest home, where tales are told,*
*Of Washington's ancestors, quiet and plain,*
*Farmers and gentry, their lives humane.*
*In Sulgrave's halls, with their weathered stone,*
*Echo the whispers of seeds once sown.*
*A lineage strong, yet humble and sure,*
*Built on values noble, steadfast, and pure.*
*The Washington crest, with its stars and bars,*
*Hinted of destinies written in stars.*

*Though oceans divided the legacy's flow,*
*The roots of his greatness began to grow.*
*From England's fields to Virginia's soil,*
*Where settlers laboured with sweat and toil,*
*The Washington name took its place,*
*In the heart of a young and hopeful race.*
*At Mount Vernon, his life would bloom,*
*A countryside haven, a leader's room.*
*With sprawling fields and a river's song,*
*It was here he pondered right and wrong.*
*The red-brick mansion, stately yet warm,*
*Weathered the sun, the winds, the storm.*
*Its gardens bloomed with nature's cheer,*
*Reflecting the man who lived here.*
*The cherry trees and the fields of grain,*
*Bore witness to triumph, to loss, to pain.*
*For Washington's heart, though stern and bold,*
*Carried a love for the simple and old.*
*The hearth at Mount Vernon's glowing light,*
*Kept him grounded in the darkest night.*
*Though battles raged and freedom called,*
*Here, his spirit was gently enthralled.*
*His hands, once raised in a general's fight,*
*Found solace in planting and tending the light.*
*The fields whispered stories of peace and toil,*
*A refuge carved from Virginia's soil.*
*Yet his thoughts would stray to a land afar,*

*Where Sulgrave Manor stood beneath English stars.*
*Did he wonder, in his quiet hours,*
*Of English meadows and ancient towers?*
*Though his loyalty lay with the land he led,*
*His ancestral ties were never dead.*
*The past and present, though oceans apart,*
*Merged like rivers within his heart.*
*As the leader of a nation's birth,*
*He cherished the land, its boundless worth.*
*But not with the lust of kings for thrones,*
*His love was humble, rooted in homes.*
*He fought not for power, but liberty's flame,*
*A guiding light, eternal in name.*
*The first to serve, the first to lead,*
*The father who planted freedom's seed.*
*And when the Revolution's storm was done,*
*When the battles were fought, the victory won,*
*He chose to return, not to power's sway,*
*But to Mount Vernon's gentle bay.*
*The plow replaced the sword he bore,*
*As he sought the peace he'd longed for.*
*Among his fields, with the sun's descent,*
*He found the life of quiet content.*
*Yet the world remembers him not for his rest,*
*But for the trials he faced, the tests.*
*At Valley Forge, through the frost and snow,*
*He led with resolve when spirits were low.*

*Across the Delaware, his courage burned,*
*A tide of freedom, the course he turned.*
*A leader, a farmer, a patriot true,*
*A man whose vision the whole world knew.*
*Now, Sulgrave stands in the English mist,*
*A reminder of a bond that persists.*
*While Mount Vernon watches the Potomac's tide,*
*Its rolling hills a nation's pride.*
*Two homes, two lands, yet one great man,*
*Whose legacy bridges where it began.*
*From humble roots to freedom's fight,*
*He shines as a star in history's night.*
*George Washington, your life, your name,*
*Is etched in time, an eternal flame.*
*From the English manor to the Virginian shore,*
*Your spirit lives on, forevermore.*
*The homes you cherished, the values you bore,*
*Will echo through history's endless roar.*

# 20. A Voyage with Darwin

*Beneath the endless azure skies,*
*Where the ocean's breath in whispers lies,*
*A solitary bird with feathers bright,*
*Embarked on a journey, guided by light.*
*Not of her choosing, nor by her plan,*
*But carried by fate and the will of man.*
*She fluttered down to the deck one day,*
*A stowaway soul in the Beagle's sway.*
*The ship, a cradle of human thought,*
*Bound for lands that the world forgot.*
*Charles Darwin stood with eyes of fire,*
*A seeker of truths, a man of desire.*
*The bird, unknowing of her role to play,*
*Perched on the mast as the ship sailed away.*
*Her wings had known the ocean's spray,*
*But now they'd bear her to a new ballet.*

***Part I: The Call of the Unknown***

*The sailors laughed at the bird of grey,*
*"An omen of luck!" they'd often say.*
*Yet she watched them with a piercing gaze,*

*Seeing their hopes, their fears, their ways.*
*In their rough hands and calloused skin,*
*She felt the pulse of the world within.*
*For men who roamed where the waves expand,*
*Held dreams as vast as the shifting sand.*
*Darwin would sit in quiet thought,*
*Sketching wonders his mind had caught.*
*From beetles small to coral reefs,*
*He wove the threads of nature's beliefs.*
*And the bird, a silent, curious guide,*
*Flew from the mast to his side.*
*She'd watch as he wrote with a steady hand,*
*Mapping the secrets of sea and land.*
*Her wings had known the storm's embrace,*
*Yet now they sought a gentler grace.*
*The ship, though bound by man's desire,*
*Sailed to realms that would inspire.*
*The bird felt in her heart the pull,*
*Of the ocean vast, mysterious, full.*
*And she wondered, as the winds did call,*
*If man's search for answers could conquer all.*

### *Part II: The Galápagos Awakens*

*When the Beagle reached the Galápagos shore,*
*The bird beheld a world to explore.*
*Islands carved by volcanic flame,*
*A raw, untouched, eternal frame.*
*Darwin marvelled at the finches' beaks,*

*At tortoises old, with wisdom that speaks.*

*Each step he took, each note he penned,*

*Was a journey begun, but not an end.*

*The bird soared high, her wings outstretched,*

*Over cliffs where iguanas basked and etched.*

*She watched as Darwin's keen eyes traced,*

*Patterns of life that the world embraced.*

*In solitude, she felt his plight,*

*A man alone in the pursuit of light.*

*For knowledge, she knew, was a heavy crown,*

*A path that could lift yet weigh one down.*

*The bird, too, felt the pangs of her heart,*

*For the ocean she left, now worlds apart.*

*The spray of the waves, the endless skies,*

*The cries of her kin, her lullabies.*

*And yet in her solitude, she found a kin,*

*In the human quest that lay within.*

*Darwin, too, had left behind,*

*A simpler world, a peaceful mind.*

### *Part III: Lessons from the Sea*

*As days turned to months on the endless tide,*

*The bird saw truths she couldn't hide.*

*Man, like her, was a wanderer too,*

*Seeking answers in the vast, the new.*

*But unlike her wings, his tools were thought,*

*With questions deep and lessons sought.*

*She saw in Darwin a mirror of fate,*

*Both travellers bound by nature's gate.*
*In the whisper of waves and the ship's groan,*
*She found a lesson, wholly her own:*
*That solitude isn't an empty cage,*
*But a place where souls can turn the page.*
*The ocean, vast and unknowable still,*
*Taught her of freedom, of nature's will.*
*And Darwin, though human, shared her plight,*
*A seeker of truths in the endless night.*
*For every island, every reef,*
*Brought him closer to belief.*
*Not of gods in the heavens above,*
*But of nature's design, its silent love.*
*The bird watched as he pieced it all,*
*The rise of life, the great and small.*
*And in her heart, she felt the swell,*
*Of truths unspoken, of tales to tell.*

### Part IV: Nostalgia's Soft Call

*Yet as the Beagle turned its bow,*
*To return to the world it left till now,*
*The bird felt a tug, a mournful ache,*
*For the home she'd left, the paths to take.*
*The ship, her haven, had shown her much,*
*Of human will, of nature's touch.*
*But now the call of her kindred rang,*
*A song of the sea, the life it sang.*
*Darwin, too, felt a weight inside,*

For England's shores and the countryside.
He longed for the quiet of familiar fields,
For the comfort his homeland yields.
Yet he knew that life had changed its tune,
For the truths he found beneath the moon.
He saw in the bird a kindred soul,
Both shaped by journeys that made them whole.

**Part V: The Eternal Flight**

When the Beagle docked, the bird took flight,
Disappearing into the fading light.
She carried with her the lessons learned,
From the ship, the man, and the worlds they turned.
Darwin watched as she soared away,
A symbol of all he'd seen on the way.
For she, like him, was a traveller still,
Bound by wonder, driven by will.
And so the bird became a lore,
A spirit of discovery forevermore.
Her wings, though small, had spanned the skies,
And carried the weight of man's great "whys."
She taught of solitude's bittersweet grace,
Of nostalgia's call and time's embrace.
And Darwin, her witness, would forever tell,
Of the bird who journeyed where wonders dwell.
For in the heart of every man,
Lies the urge to wander, to understand.
The bird and Darwin, two lives entwined,

*Remind us of the beauty we seek to find.*
*Through oceans vast and skies unknown,*
*Through solitude's ache and nostalgia's tone,*
*We are all travellers, on paths untold,*
*Seeking nature's secrets, worth more than gold.*
*And so the bird, though gone from view,*
*Flies in the hearts of the seekers, the true.*
*Her journey, her lessons, her silent lore,*
*Live on in the quest for forevermore.*

# 21. The Artful Tongue

*Oh, language shaped like molten glass,*
*Refined, precise, where few dare pass,*
*Each word a gem, each phrase a stone,*
*A world of thought in Joyce's tone.*
*Through Dubliners, the city breathes,*
*Its life etched deep, like autumn leaves.*
*A tongue both tough and supple wrought,*
*A web of meaning, finely caught.*
*Joyce, the smith of English flame,*
*Chiselled words that none could tame.*
*A master of cadence, rhythm, and sound,*
*In his prose, humanity's truths abound.*
*No simple tongue, no careless flair,*
*But crafted lines with weight and care.*
*From common speech to grand refrain,*
*Each sentence carries life's refrain.*
*The Language of Grit and Grace*
*In dusty pubs and shadowed lanes,*
*The voices rise, their joys, their pains.*
*Each syllable sharp, with edges rough,*
*The Dublin tongue, unyielding, tough.*
*Yet laced with wit, and raw desire,*

*A spark of humour, a flickering fire.*
*Through every tale, a world unfolds,*
*Of broken dreams and hearts grown cold.*
*The rhythm of Dublin's streets and sky,*
*Finds its soul in Joyce's cry.*
*No polished veneer, no soft disguise,*
*But truth reflected in weary eyes.*
*The language dares, it cuts, it stings,*
*It soars with eagles, then clips their wings.*
*It bends like light, through glass and rain,*
*A prism of joy, of loss, of pain.*

**Stories as Mirrors of the Soul**

*Through Eveline, her heart's unrest,*
*The weight of choice upon her chest.*
*The language falters, caught in pause,*
*To show the ache of unwritten laws.*
*Or Gabriel's pride in "The Dead,"*
*With words like whispers, heavy as lead.*
*The snow falls softly, thick and white,*
*Binding all lives in its quiet might.*
*In "Araby," youth's fragile hope,*
*Caught in the shadow of life's vast scope,*
*The language shifts, from soft to stark,*
*Dreams extinguished in the dark.*
*The mundane world, the holy quest,*
*Each phrase a symbol, each thought expressed.*
*From fleeting lust to faith betrayed,*

*Joyce's words make the fleeting stay.*
### The Toughness of Truth
*Joyce's English, a granite wall,*
*A fortress built to hold it all.*
*Its toughness lies in how it speaks,*
*Not for the shallow, but the deep it seeks.*
*Words that challenge, that question, that claim,*
*Every character, their guilt and shame.*
*He holds no hand, he spares no blow,*
*The world's raw truths in his language flow.*
*Yet within its rigor, beauty hides,*
*A quiet grace in the ebbing tides.*
*The music of life, its highs and lows,*
*In Joyce's prose, its rhythm flows.*
*He speaks of Dublin, small and gray,*
*But his words expand, take flight, convey.*
*The universal in the local seen,*
*Through every shadow, a light serene.*
### Refined Through Fire
*The fire of thought, the forge of art,*
*Burned brightly in Joyce's heart.*
*Each word, a fragment of his design,*
*Polished, tempered, by the grind of time.*
*Not just a tale, but a canvas wide,*
*Where emotion and intellect coincide.*
*The roughness of life, the sharpest edge,*
*Carved into language, a living pledge.*

*His sentences twist, their meaning deep,*
*They dance awake, they murmur, they weep.*
*A writer's craft, honed razor-sharp,*
*Language like music, prose like a harp.*
*The challenge, the beauty, the unspoken pain,*
*Echo in the reader's brain.*
*The English tongue, so tough, so bright,*
*Made infinite under Joyce's light.*

### Lessons of Dubliners

*What can we learn from Joyce's tongue,*
*From the songs of Dublin he deftly sung?*
*That life's truth lies in the mundane,*
*In small frustrations and quiet pain.*
*That language, refined, can elevate,*
*Even the simplest tales of fate.*
*That beauty dwells in the grit of days,*
*In the human heart, in its endless maze.*
*So raise a toast to James Joyce's art,*
*A master of craft, a breaker of hearts.*
*Through Dubliners, his city stands,*
*A testament to life's rough hands.*
*The English language, through his prose,*
*Became a garden where thought still grows.*
*Tough and refined, like steel and flame,*
*Forever etched is Joyce's name.*

# 22. Meeting Wilde!

*In Merrion Square, where whispers hum,*

*Where lilacs bloom and poets come,*

*The shadows dance in morning's gold,*

*And tales of Dublin's heart are told.*

*It's here, among the ancient trees,*

*That time breathes soft, on memories.*

*I walked the path where roots entwined,*

*With Dublin's past, both fierce and kind.*

*And there, beneath the cedar's shade,*

*A figure lingered, finely made.*

*A man in coat of velvet green,*

*With wit as sharp as eyes serene.*

*His gaze was fixed on something near,*

*A daisy trembling, pure and clear.*

*He plucked it gently, lips half-curved,*

*As if its beauty he deserved.*

*I stood in awe; could it be true?*

*That Wilde himself had come to view?*

### The Spark of Words

*"Good morning, sir," I dared to say,*

*"What brings you here this cloudless day?"*

*He turned, his smile a wicked art,*

*As if he'd read my beating heart.*
*"My dear," he mused, with lilting tone,*
*"The Square's alive, though made of stone.*
*Each leaf, each blade, each tender vine,*
*Is but a verse of life's design.*
*Why would one choose to stay indoors,*
*When Dublin sings from all her pores?"*
*His voice was honey, warm and bright,*
*A playwright's charm, a poet's light.*

### On Dublin, Life, and Art

*"Do you know," he asked, his eyes aglow,*
*"What makes this city's beauty grow?*
*It's not the bricks, the walls, the streets,*
*But hearts like yours that life completes.*
*Dublin's laughter, its pain, its song,*
*It made me wise, it made me strong."*
*He paused, and glanced at distant spires,*
*His voice now softer, filled with fires.*
*"Though England crowned me with disdain,*
*It's Dublin's spirit I retain.*
*For here, amidst this park's embrace,*
*I first knew beauty's truest face.*
*The wit, the wine, the rebel's charm,*
*The Irish soul, so fierce, so warm.*
*And Merrion Square, this sacred space,*
*Holds memories no time can erase."*

### A Meeting of Origins

*I felt the roots beneath my feet,*
*The tethered bond, the moment sweet.*
*"I was born here," I softly said,*
*"My first breath where these paths are spread."*
*He smiled, as if the thought was dear,*
*"Then you, my friend, belong here."*
*"You've Dublin's soul within your veins,*
*Its joys, its sorrows, its tender pains.*
*Guard it well, this gift of lore,*
*For few are born of Merrion Square."*
*I felt his words like threads of gold,*
*A fabric spun from tales of old.*

### Parting Shadows

*He turned to leave, the moment brief,*
*Like twilight's glow, a fragile thief.*
*But as he went, his shadow stayed,*
*A silhouette the sun had made.*
*"Remember this," he called to me,*
*"True beauty lies in being free.*
*No chain of fame, no gilded throne,*
*Can match the heart that's truly known.*
*Speak boldly, live, and write your truth,*
*And keep forever Dublin's youth."*
*The air grew still, the park a stage,*
*As Wilde departed, page by page.*
*And though the years may sweep away,*
*That meeting holds, its vivid sway.*

*For Merrion Square, with blooms adorned,*
*Still hums with Wilde, and dreams reborn.*
*In every petal, every tree,*
*His spirit lingers, wild and free.*

# 23. Jerusalem

*Beneath the sun's eternal blaze,*
*Where time dissolves in golden haze,*
*Jerusalem stands, a sacred throne,*
*Of stone and story, flesh and bone.*
*A city carved by hands divine,*
*Where earth and heaven intertwine.*
*Its walls hold whispers, ancient, deep,*
*Of prayers uttered, of wounds that seep.*
*The olive trees, their branches grey,*
*Have watched empires rise and fade away.*
*The stones of Zion, rough and old,*
*Bear witness to tales the ages told.*
*Each step you take on her hallowed ground,*
*Echoes with voices, profound, unbound.*
*Jerusalem, a beacon, bright,*
*Where shadows meet eternal light.*
*Here, Abraham's faith took its flight,*
*A promise born beneath the starlit night.*
*The Mount of Moriah, where he stood still,*
*Binding his son to divine will.*
*And David, the shepherd, with heart so bold,*
*Dreamt of a city of prophets foretold.*

*From the Ark's ascent to Solomon's shrine,*
*The Temple rose, both mortal and divine.*
*For the children of Israel, this land was home,*
*A kingdom eternal beneath the dome.*
*But tides of conquest, wars of dust,*
*Shook the city's foundations, turned hope to rust.*
*Yet through the ruins, the faithful prayed,*
*Their covenant strong, their spirit stayed.*
*Then came the Prophet, born to speak,*
*Of love and peace, of the humble and meek.*
*Christ walked her streets, beneath her sky,*
*Preaching a truth that would never die.*
*Gethsemane wept for the sin of the world,*
*As the weight of a cross on His back unfurled.*
*And Calvary's hill bore witness to pain,*
*As blood fell like cleansing rain.*
*From Jerusalem's heart, the crescent rose,*
*A call to prayer in its twilight glows.*
*The Dome of the Rock, in splendour gleams,*
*Where Prophet dreamed celestial dreams.*
*The Night Journey carried his soul to the skies,*
*Uniting the faithful beneath almighty eyes.*
*Three faiths converge, their stories entwine,*
*A testament to the sacred, the divine.*
*Each stone in her walls, a voice, a plea,*
*Of yearning hearts, of history.*
*The Western Wall, where tears are shed,*

*For the Temple destroyed, for the lives now dead.*
*Pilgrims press their hands to the cold,*
*And slip between the cracks their prayers untold.*
*Above, the golden dome does gleam,*
*A vision of hope, a shared dream.*
*The Via Dolorosa, the path of grief,*
*Winds through the streets, sharp and brief.*
*The burden of history weighs so deep,*
*On the steps where the faithful softly weep.*
*The Church of the Holy Sepulchre stands,*
*Built by devotion, shaped by hands.*
*A sacred tomb, a place to kneel,*
*Where humanity's wounds begin to heal.*
*The Mount of Olives watches the night,*
*A sentinel draped in soft moonlight.*
*Its graves hold secrets, its winds still hum,*
*With the echoes of prophecies yet to come.*
*And from its crest, the city unfolds,*
*A tapestry woven with threads of gold.*
*Jerusalem, O city of peace,*
*Why does your strife never cease?*
*Your streets have known both sword and flame,*
*Empires rise and fall in your name.*
*From Babylon's chains to Rome's iron fist,*
*Your story is one of a ceaseless twist.*
*Crusaders marched, their banners high,*
*To claim the city where saints did lie.*

*Saladin's wisdom, his measured hand,*
*Brought justice to this fractured land.*
*But still the wars and hatred reign,*
*A cycle of loss, of endless pain.*
*Jerusalem, torn by greed and zeal,*
*A wound too deep for time to heal.*
*Yet amidst the blood, the prayers, the strife,*
*Hope endures, like the pulse of life.*
*Oh Jerusalem, your beauty glows,*
*In dawn's first light, in twilight's close.*
*Your streets are narrow, your markets loud,*
*Your skies are vast, your spirit proud.*
*The spices linger in the air,*
*The call to prayer floats soft and fair.*
*Your people, though broken, though torn apart,*
*Still carry your name within their heart.*
*Through narrow lanes, where stories meet,*
*Each turn unveils a history complete.*
*The Armenian Quarter, cloaked in grace,*
*Keeps its culture in this sacred space.*
*The Jewish Quarter hums with song,*
*A testament to enduring strong.*
*The Christian bells, the muezzin's call,*
*Echo together above the wall.*

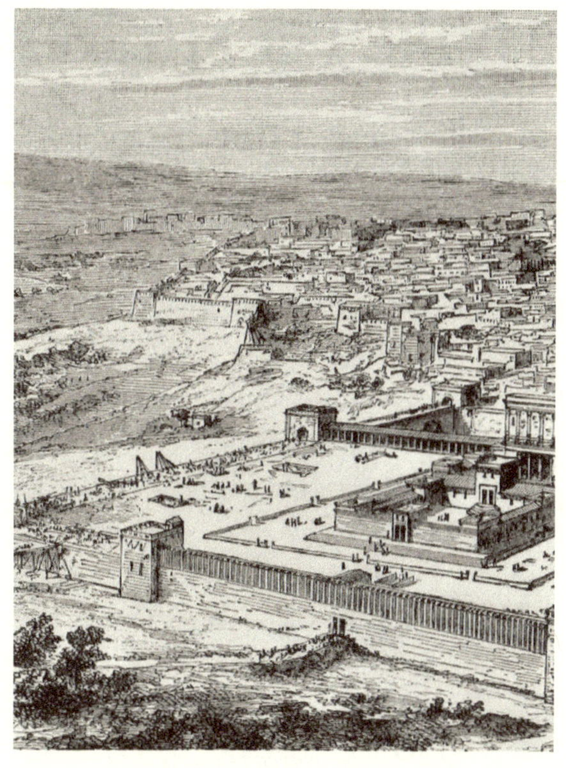

# 24. The Tale of Taxila

*On the banks where the Indus flows,*
*Where the winds of time in silence blow,*
*Lies a city of ruins, proud and old,*
*A story of glory, of riches untold.*
*Taxila, where wisdom once did reign,*
*In the dust of centuries, it will remain.*
*From ancient mouths, its name did call,*
*A cradle of knowledge, revered by all.*

**The Dawn of Taxila**

*Long before the empires rose,*
*Before the ink of history froze,*
*There stood a city, proud and bright,*
*Bathed in the golden morning light.*
*The Aryan wanderers found their way,*
*Through mountain passes, at break of day.*
*On the fertile plains, they built with care,*
*A city destined for wisdom rare.*
*Taxila, where knowledge bloomed,*
*Where sages spoke and ideas loomed,*
*A crossroads of cultures, of east and west,*
*Where philosophers put their minds to the test.*
*From Persia to Greece, from India's heart,*

*The city gathered, and played its part.*
*Trade and thought, both intertwined,*
*In Taxila, where all could find.*
*In the shadow of the mountains high,*
*Where the eagles soar and the rivers sigh,*
*The scholars gathered, their minds ablaze,*
*In Taxila's halls, through ancient days.*
*The students came, from far and wide,*
*To learn of the world, and to cast aside,*
*The ignorance that chained them tight,*
*To see the world in a clearer light.*
*Aryabhata, the mathematic sage,*
*Studied the stars, and the cosmic stage.*
*In the great libraries, scrolls were spread,*
*Of science, of art, of knowledge dead.*
*Gurus and sages, their minds refined,*
*Brought teachings from distant lands, aligned.*
*Aristotle's philosophy met Indian thought,*
*In Taxila, where wisdom was sought.*
*Gandhara's art in the markets spilled,*
*Crafted by hands with patience skilled.*
*The Greco-Buddhist union bloomed,*
*A fusion of cultures, an era groomed.*
*In the temples, silence echoed deep,*
*While traders bargained and secrets keep.*
*But in the temples, in every shrine,*
*A seed of knowledge began to shine.*

### *The Rise of Empires*

*The city stood with gates so wide,*
*Where empires sought, and dreams did collide.*
*The Persians came, with fire in their eyes,*
*They marched through fields, beneath the skies.*
*Darius, the king, with his vast command,*
*Led his forces across the land.*
*Taxila's wealth, so rich and bright,*
*A jewel in the emperor's sight.*
*But the city, as always, stood strong and tall,*
*Resilient through every rise and fall.*
*It was not just gold, but minds it fed,*
*In each brick, a lesson was said.*
*The Greeks arrived with Alexander's might,*
*Their soldiers bright, their hearts alight.*
*But it was in Taxila's heart they knew,*
*That the conquest of minds would see them through.*
*Alexander himself, with eyes so keen,*
*Studied the wisdom that could be seen.*
*In the scrolls, in the books, in the sages' lore,*
*The city gave more than they could explore.*
*A place of great learning, as legends told,*
*Where the world's first scholars took their hold.*
*Through this ancient city's gates they passed,*
*Leaving footprints in the sands that last.*

### *The Glory of the Mauryas*

*Then came the Maurya dynasty's rise,*

*Ashoka, the king, with vision wise.*
*From the east, he brought his reign,*
*Bringing peace to the land again.*
*Taxila's gates welcomed him in,*
*A ruler of compassion, who would begin,*
*To spread the word of Buddha's path,*
*Through wisdom's teachings and peaceful wrath.*
*In Taxila, the Buddha's word was heard,*
*And the city's heart began to stir.*
*A place of worship, of quiet prayer,*
*Where monks would meditate without despair.*
*Ashoka's empire, vast and grand,*
*Lifted Taxila to heights so planned.*
*A jewel in the heart of the empire's chest,*
*Taxila was now among the best.*
*But as all things rise, they also fall,*
*And the winds of change would soon call.*
*The great Maurya dynasty was torn,*
*And from their ashes, a new world was born.*
*Taxila's light dimmed with each war,*
*As the winds of fortune closed the door.*
*The city once proud, now buried deep,*
*In the rubble of time, it went to sleep.*

### The Decline and Fall

*The centuries passed, and the winds did change,*
*As rulers clashed and empires ranged.*
*Huns and Persians, through the gates they came,*

*Taxila burned, a hollowed name.*
*The temples crumbled, the schools fell silent,*
*The sages' words lost, now violent.*
*The markets ceased, the roads grew still,*
*And the city that once stood proud, fell ill.*
*What once was bright, now lay in dust,*
*A place where even time could not trust.*
*But in the hearts of those who knew,*
*Taxila's spirit forever grew.*
*For knowledge lost is never gone,*
*It lies within, and carries on.*
*Though ruins remain and shadows loom,*
*The light of learning will still bloom.*

### The Modern Dream

*Today, in the fields where ruins lie,*
*The winds still whisper, the eagles fly.*
*Taxila, though broken, still holds its grace,*
*A sacred memory in time's embrace.*
*The scholars come, and pilgrims too,*
*To see the place where wisdom grew.*
*The stones may crumble, the walls decay,*
*But Taxila's story will never fade away.*
*A city of thought, a city of fire,*
*Its legacy remains, its heart, its desire,*
*To teach, to learn, to never cease,*
*To find in knowledge, eternal peace.*
*And though the world may turn away,*

*Taxila's light will always stay.*
*A city of scholars, a city of dream,*
*Where time and wisdom forever stream.*

### *The Enduring Flame*

*Taxila, O city of forgotten past,*
*Your name will echo, your memory last.*
*Through centuries lost, through empires crushed,*
*Your spirit rises, never hushed.*
*For in your dust, your bones, your stone,*
*Lies the beating heart of what's been sown.*
*A testament to those who seek,*
*The knowledge that will make them free.*
*So let the winds through ruins sweep,*
*Let the city's song forever keep,*
*In the hearts of those who dare to learn,*
*The flame of Taxila will always burn.*
*A place of greatness, of truth and strife,*
*Taxila, the city that gave us life.*

# 25. Dublin, City of Heavy Skies

*In the grey of dawn, the city wakes,*
*A silence deep that nothing breaks,*
*The cobblestones, they weep in rain,*
*As shadows drift through streets of pain.*
*The Liffey's flow, so cold and clear,*
*Carries the whispers of yesteryear,*
*Of dreams long lost, of songs unsung,*
*Of days when hope was young.*
*Dublin, O city of heavy skies,*
*Where every soul with sadness sighs,*
*Beneath your arches, ghosts still roam,*
*In search of what they once called home.*
*The pubs are full, yet hearts are bare,*
*A city rich with vacant air.*
*For in the laughter, there's a tear,*
*A pain that lingers, year to year.*

### The Streets Remember

*Your streets are lined with memories worn,*
*Like torn old pages, weathered and torn.*
*The doors are shut, the windows closed,*

*Yet something stirs, something composed.*
*The children laugh, yet can't quite see,*
*The sorrow carved in history.*
*The songs of Yeats, the cries of Joyce,*
*Resound like ghosts without a voice.*
*The spires of churches, they stand tall,*
*But no prayer rises, no angels call.*
*The bells that ring, they sing of loss,*
*Of hope buried under endless cross.*
*Each step on O'Connell Bridge feels lost,*
*As if the city counts its cost.*
*The streets that knew both joy and cheer,*
*Now hold only echoes of forgotten years.*

### The Heart of Dublin

*Oh Dublin, your heart beats slow and faint,*
*Painted in shades of blue and taint.*
*Where once the fire of life did burn,*
*Now ashes fall, and none return.*
*The memories haunt the empty lanes,*
*The laughter lost, the love in chains.*
*The River Liffey flows with pride,*
*Yet hides the tears the city hides.*
*Your castles, old, stand proud in vain,*
*Worn by time, by winds, by rain.*
*And though the parks are green and wide,*
*Beneath the grass, the roots still bide.*
*The ghosts of lovers, the ghosts of kings,*

*Their whispers caught on broken wings.*
*Dublin, O city, your heart is torn,*
*Between the night and the coming morn.*

### The Haunting of the Mind

*I wander through your ancient lanes,*
*Where once was joy now only pains.*
*The laughter's gone, replaced by doubt,*
*The songs are hushed, the dreams snuffed out.*
*The past that clung, now slips away,*
*Like fleeting clouds at close of day.*
*But in the silence, I hear your call,*
*A cry that echoes through the hall.*
*The faces pass, but none they smile,*
*The city's charm, gone out of style.*
*You stand in ruins, proud but grey,*
*A fading star at end of day.*
*And yet, in every empty street,*
*There's something haunting, bittersweet.*
*The spirit of a place once bright,*
*Now lost in shadows, far from light.*

### The Unspoken Tears

*Oh Dublin, the tears you do not speak,*
*For every sorrow that feels so weak.*
*The city hums a mournful song,*
*Of where it's been, of what went wrong.*
*The stories linger, never told,*
*Of battles fought and hearts grown cold.*

*The winds of time have swept them past,*
*But Dublin holds them, steadfast, fast.*
*The trees in St. Stephen's Green stand tall,*
*But under their boughs, shadows fall.*
*The world may move, but you remain,*
*A city washed in endless rain.*
*Your beauty is a lonesome cry,*
*A fading hope beneath the sky.*
*And though you stand, you do not smile,*
*For Dublin, dear, has lost its style.*

### The City's Soul

*But somewhere, deep within your bones,*
*Is something more than empty stones.*
*A city built on dreams and woe,*
*Where past and present softly flow.*
*Your soul, though weary, still is strong,*
*A mournful, sweet, and endless song.*
*For though the tears may dim your eyes,*
*You'll rise again, beneath the skies.*
*Yet, Dublin, O city, my heart does break,*
*For all the promises you could not make.*
*The years may pass, and time may wane,*
*But you will live, and you'll remain.*
*In every corner, in every street,*
*In every loss, in every beat,*
*You'll carry the weight of what once was,*
*A city forever lost in pause.*

*And still, beneath your shadowed skies,*
*The heart of Dublin never dies.*
*Though torn and battered, bruised and bare,*
*You'll rise again from dark despair.*
*For in your depths, your soul is found,*
*A quiet peace, a mournful sound.*
*Dublin, O city of tears and pride,*
*Your sorrow is the place where dreams abide.*

# 26. The Ship That Sails on Land

*A ship that sails, not on the sea,*

*But on the earth, where none can see,*

*Its hull of dreams, its mast of hope,*

*It sails through skies, it never moors.*

*Beneath the sun, across the sand,*

*The ship it sails, but can't expand,*

*Its sails, they flutter, wild and free,*

*Yet it cannot touch the endless sea.*

*It rides the waves of distant thought,*

*Of love and loss, of battles fought.*

*A ship that moves where none have been,*

*It longs to touch, but can't be seen.*

*It searches shores, it finds no home,*

*It seeks for lands where hearts might roam,*

*But ports are distant, shores unseen,*

*The ship must sail, forever keen.*

*It whispers in the winds of night,*

*Of love once kind, now lost to light.*

*The shores it dreams of, far away,*

*No matter how it sails, won't stay.*

*The ship it craves what cannot be,*
*A love that's pure, that's wild and free.*
*Yet even in the winds that blow,*
*The truth is clear, it cannot go.*
*It sails on fields where flowers fade,*
*Through valleys deep, through skies that trade,*
*The stars above, they look away,*
*For in its course, they cannot stay.*
*It sails where no one dares to dream,*
*It chases shadows, flickers, gleam.*
*And yet it moves, though all is lost,*
*A ship whose path is bound by cost.*
*The winds may change, the tides may rise,*
*But all it seeks is far from sight,*
*For ships that sail on earth alone,*
*Can never reach the heart, the throne.*
*A ship that sails, yet never lands,*
*It yearns for hearts, but slips like sands.*
*It builds its dreams with fragile wood,*
*Of what it wants, of what it could.*
*But love is not a course to chart,*
*It's not a ship with sails to start.*
*It's in the earth, it's in the skies,*
*It's in the truth behind the lies.*
*The ship will sail, its journey's long,*
*Yet still it searches, still it's strong.*
*For even in the winds it cries,*

*It knows that love can never die.*
*It moves, but anchored, never stays,*
*A fleeting thought in misted haze.*
*The ship is free, but bound to roam,*
*Seeking love that's far from home.*
*It sails the deserts, climbs the hills,*
*It moves, but never stills its will.*
*For love is not a course to take,*
*It's something more than ships can make.*
*And so it sails on, winds that weep,*
*A ship that yearns, yet cannot keep.*
*The love it seeks is far away,*
*Beyond the reach of night and day.*
*And still the ship, it sails the land,*
*With empty heart and steady hand.*
*It searches for what cannot stay,*
*A love that drifts too far away.*
*It sails in silence, through the night,*
*A shadow lost to fading light.*
*It knows no end, it knows no start,*
*It's caught between the mind and heart.*
*For ships that sail in search of love,*
*Will never find what they dream of.*
*They travel far, yet never touch,*
*The things they seek, they crave too much.*
*A ship that sails but cannot land,*
*On soil so rich, yet barren sand,*

*A heart that loves but cannot stay,*
*Forever chasing, drifting away.*
*For love is not a place to find,*
*It's in the fleeting of the mind.*
*A ship may sail, but it will roam,*
*For in its course, it's always home.*
*It moves through seasons, through the years,*
*A ship that sails through quiet fears.*
*Its journey endless, wild and wide,*
*In search of love it cannot hide.*
*A ship that sails upon the earth,*
*A dream too grand, a soul of worth.*
*But in the end, it cannot stay,*
*For love's a ship that sails away.*

# About The Author

An avid wordsmith and dreamer, Sowparnika Nair of Delhi Public School Bangalore East, is a high school enchantress whose heart finds solace in the rhythm of poetry. With a pen that dances like a whispering breeze, she weaves emotions into verses, painting vivid landscapes of hope and introspection. Guided by the enchanting power of language, Sowparnika aspires to create a symphony of words that resonates with the hearts of all who wander through her verses.